One Hundred and One Things You Should
Never Ask A Marine
To Do

Fifth Edition

By Ed Temple

Marine Corps-Law Enforcement Foundation, Inc.
10 Rockefeller Plaza
Suite 1007
New York, NY 10020

Certified as one of America's Best Charities by **Independent Charities of America**, MC-LEF makes scholarships, bonds and special medical assistance possible through generous support of individuals and corporations. Attend a formal gala or golf tournament, establish a memorial or honorary scholarship, donate stocks or assets, or include the foundation in your will. The MC-LEF helps families who have sacrificed so much to serve and protect our communities and our country.

Please make checks payable to: Marine Corps-Law Enforcement Foundation

Marine Corps-Law Enforcement Foundation, Inc. is registered to participate in the Combined Federal Campaign (CFC #10507).

We are a 501(c)3 charity, IRS tax number 22-3357410.

tel: 877-606-1775 fax: 973-625-9239

www.mc-lef.org   e-mail: info@mc-lef.org

Dedicated to
my wife Pamela, for your
love, support and tolerance.

To my daughters
Barbara and Karen.

In Memory of

those Marines that gave their
lives in the headquarters bombing of 1983
in Beirut, Lebanon.

The streets of Heaven are peaceful, serene.
Guarded by another, U.S. MARINE.

Never ask a Marine to go grocery shopping.

Never ask a Marine to go fishing.

Never ask a Marine to give a short speech.

Never ask a Marine to stop a leaky faucet.

Never ask a Marine to take that hill.

Never ask a Marine to go bird watching.

Never ask a Marine to go to a drive-in movie.

Never ask a Marine to work in intensive care.

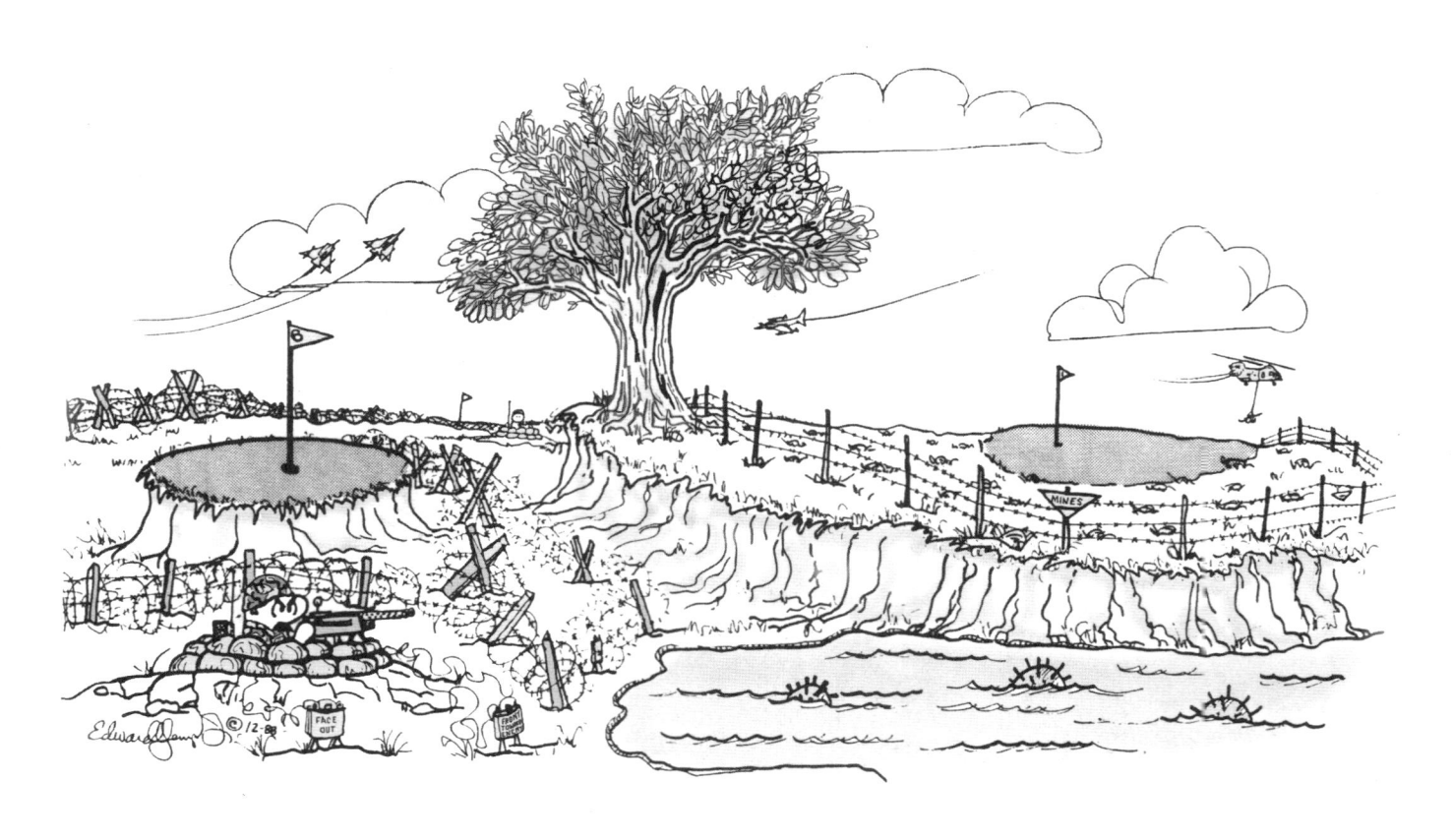

Never ask a Marine to build a golf course.

Never ask a Marine to make hamburger meat.

Never ask a Woman Marine to be a fashion designer.

Never ask a Marine to be a used car salesman.

Never ask a Marine to shoot pool.

Never ask a Marine to install a burglar alarm.

Never ask a Marine to tell you where sand fleas come from.

Never ask a Marine to wash windows.

Never ask a Marine to lift weights.

Never ask a Marine to be a farmer.

Never ask a Marine to help move your house.

Never ask a Marine to make lemonade.

Never ask a Marine to build a playground.

Never ask a Marine to get a drivers license.

Never ask a Marine to be a lifeguard.

Never ask a Marine to plant things around the yard.

Never ask a Marine to load a ship.

Never ask a Marine to drop by for the weekend.

Never ask a Marine to give you a back massage.

Never ask a Marine to go to a drive-thru restaurant.

Never ask an Old Marine to tell you about the OLD CORPS.

Never ask a Marine to tell you about *@%%$#* mistakes.

Never ask a Marine to go fox hunting.

Never ask a Marine to cut down trees.

Never ask a Marine to play video games.

Never ask a Marine to paint your house.

Never ask a Marine to call for help.

Never ask a Marine to shovel snow.

Never ask a Marine to clean out your garage.

Never ask a Marine to be a tailor.

Never ask a Marine to wax your car.

Never ask a Marine to play hide-n-seek.

Never ask a Marine to fix your kid's tricycle tire.

Never ask a Marine to run a casino.

Never ask a Marine why promotions are so slow.

Never ask a Marine to do laundry.

Never ask a Marine to dry clothes.

Never ask a Marine to cut your hair.

Never ask a Marine to come to a pool party.

Never ask a Marine to be a make-up artist.

Never ask a Marine to clean your car.

Never ask a Marine to give you directions.

Never ask a Marine to fill a prescription.

Never ask a Marine to design new weapons.

Never ask a Marine to work in a nursing home.

Never ask a Marine to play shell games.

Never ask a Marine to cut your grass.

Never ask a Marine to go on a bike hike.

Never ask a Marine to be a dietician.

Never ask a Marine to tell you where he gets his flu shot.

Never ask a Marine to put on tatoos.

Never ask a Marine to a beer party.

Never ask a Marine to go duck hunting.

Never ask a Marine to plan a short run.

Never ask a Marine to baby sit.

Never ask a Marine to play basketball.

Never ask a Marine to go to the beach.

Never ask a Marine to go to a swap meet.

Never ask a Marine to walk your dog.

Never ask a Marine to lend you a comb.

Never ask a Marine to get your cat down from a tree.

Never ask a Marine to make a daredevil jump.

Never ask a Marine to design eyeglasses.

Never ask a Marine to go bowling.

Never ask a Marine to go waterskiing.

Never ask a Marine to file an accident report.

Never ask a Marine to go mountain climbing.

Never ask a Marine to play catch.

Never ask a Marine to herd cattle.

Never ask a Marine to cook at a barbeque.

Never ask a Marine to plan a vacation cruise.

Never ask a Marine to pay a toll.

Never ask a Marine to pick you up for a date.

Never ask a Marine to read a bedtime story.

Never ask a Marine to water your lawn.

Never ask a Marine for a light.

Never ask a Marine to plan a new community.

Never ask a Marine to a formal dinner.

Never ask a Marine to kill a fly.

Never ask a Marine to go on a family picnic.

Never ask a Marine to run mass transportation.

Never ask a Marine to be an air traffic controller.

Never ask a Marine to adjust your television.

Never ask a Marine Recruiter to tell you about BOOT CAMP.

Never ask a Marine to share his dental floss.

Never ask a Woman Marine to go on a blind date.

Never ask a Marine to clean a park.

Never ask a Marine to give you a lift.

Never ask a Marine to be patient in a traffic jam.

Never ask a Marine to repair foreign cars.

Never ask a Marine to steal second base.

Never ask a Marine to give your kid a balloon ride.

Never ask this Marine to draw another 101 Things You Should Never Ask a Marine to Do.